T0171256

Brush Creek Boyhood Days

By John Alford

Order this book online at www.trafford.com
or email orders@trafford.com

Most Trafford titles are also available at major online book retailers.

Note for Librarians: A cataloguing record for this book is available from Library
and Archives Canada at www.collectionscanada.ca/amicus/index-e.html

Printed in Victoria, BC, Canada.

ISBN: 978-1-4269-2152-0 (sc)

*Our mission is to efficiently provide the world's finest, most
comprehensive book publishing service, enabling every author to
experience success. To find out how to publish your book, your way, and
have it available worldwide, visit us online at www.trafford.com*

Trafford rev. 12/22/2009

 www.trafford.com

North America & international
toll-free: 1 888 232 4444 (USA & Canada)
phone: 250 383 6864 ♦ fax: 812 355 4082

Brush Creel Boyhood Days

Jewels of Days Past

MEMORIES

By John Alford

Illustrations by Lillie Kinder

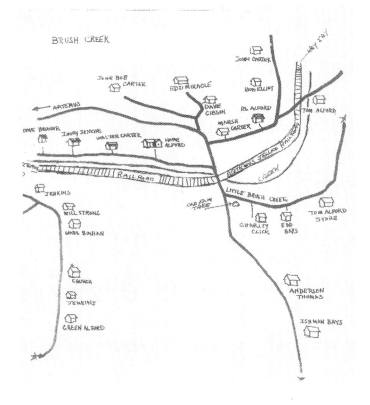

BRUSH CREEK

JOHN CARTER

HAY TOP

JOHN BOB CARTER

EDD MIRACLE

BOB ELLIOT

ARTEMUS

DAVE GIBSON

P.L. ALFORD

TOM ALFORD

MARSH CARTER

DAVE BRUNER

IVORY JENKINS

WALTER CARTER

HOME ALFORD

ARTEMUS JELLICO RAILROAD

CREEK

JENKINS

RAIL ROAD

LITTLE BRUSH CREEK

OLD ELM TREE

WILL STRONG

CHARLEY CLICK

EDD BAYS

TOM ALFORD STORE

WADE BUCHAN

CHURCH

JENKINS

ANDERSON THOMAS

GREEN ALFORD

ISHMAN BAYS

vi

Introduction

To my family: Lois (my wife), Children: John and Brenda, and the good friends that I've met in church, especially Patsy Burnette and Lillie Kinder, who have encouraged me in this endeavor. Brush Creek, where I grew up is like many of the rural areas in Southeastern Kentucky. The setting took place in the 1930's thru the late 1940's. During this time we were without many of the conveniences that most families enjoy today. We had running water when it rained and the only place is ran through was through the yard which was absent of grass. No grass was really a blessing because the only lawn mowers we had were cows. Inside plumbing was another convenience that we did not have, but it was considered a real luxury if you were fortunate to have an outhouse. It was lots of fun on Halloween night to secretly turn over the neighbors' outhouse after making quite sure that it wasn't in use. Of course you had to watch your step during this maneuver.

Electricity for lights was another convenience, which was overcome with the use of kerosene lamps. These lamps were often referred to as coal oil lamps. These worked very well except around children and cows. I had an opportunity to work for a neighbor plowing corn with a mule. At noon time, the neighbor brought me some drinking water, thinking that he had washed the vessel clean. It is very difficult to remove the scent of coal oil from any vessel. I often thought that he purposely did this to keep me from eating a big dinner.

Doing the laundry was inconvenient unless of course you were fortunate enough to have a rub board. Every lady of the house considered these a necessity for scrubbing the soil out of clothing. One gentleman in our community stated that he always bought his wife a new rub board and hoe for Christmas. Now that was thoughtful of him.

Transportation was very limited. Our mode of transportation consisted of a mule and wagon. We had a railroad that ran through Brush Creek on which they used a vehicle called a jitney. This vehicle made three or four trips a day so we could easily go to Artemus or Kay Jay.

The media consisted of the Grit Newspaper. If you remember the Grit Newspaper, the news was usually two to three weeks late, but didn't matter to us; it was still news. The other source of news was a battery radio however we children were restricted to using it. In our home, the use was for news, which was a rarity, and The Grand Ole' Opry on Saturday night. On Sunday, Cadell's Tabernacle, a fine Christian program, aired. This type of environment I now consider jewels in the rough. Where else today can an area be found with no stealing, no murder, no raping, or mayhem?

Contents

Chapter 1

My Family

My family was composed of my: Father, Mother, one Brother, and one Sister. My parents were very strict, and very often liberal in applying the rod for correction. However, sometimes an example was used. There is one that I remember quite vividly. We children were assigned chores that we were required to do. My assigned chore was that sufficient kindling wood was gathered for building fires in the cook stove and fireplace each morning. Every day when I got home from school, I was taught to put on my work clothes and do my chores. One evening, I omitted my instructions and began to play with the neighbor children next door. Soon it got quite dark and I was unable to carry out my chore. During the night, it turned rather cold. About five o'clock the next morning, I was rudely awakened and reminded that I had forgotten to do something. This example remained with me for some time.

The mechanics of home life in my day would be considered a slave life. Today one only has to adjust the thermostat for heat, flick the switch for light, dial up the oven, or push the handle to flush. I will never forget going to the outhouse on a cold, frosty morning. However, we survived with some wonderful and not so wonderful memories.

I still count my blessings when I look back and remember those times. We in America should be overjoyed with all the conveniences that we have today.

Our house was a wooden frame structure, consisting of four rooms; kitchen, dining room, and two bedrooms. The dining room was the largest room in the house. Often on Sundays, the preacher would be invited to dine with us. This didn't set well with my brother and me. We were instructed not to eat as heartily as we normally did. The both of us could easily eat a large frying chicken with all the trimmings. As we sat down at the table one Sunday, my father asked the preacher to say the blessing. Well, after about ten minutes, my brother spoke up, "Father! Tell the preacher to say Amen." After dinner I asked my brother why! He would do such a thing. He said, "When the preacher thanked the Lord for the egg that the chicken was hatched from, it was time to stop." Later that evening, after the preacher had left, my father didn't ask "Why?" he just applied means of correction. Boys will be boys.

Chapter 2

Liberty Baptist Church

When God instituted the church, He unified the family. Liberty Baptist Church as I recall was a refuge in the storm of life. Practically all the families in the area attended church. The local church, as far back as I can remember, did not have a sign out front. If different faiths attended they integrated right in with the Baptist. One fellow in particular, of the Pentecost faith,

Mr. Click never missed a service. About half way through the service, Mr. Click would begin to shout with all the Baptist saying "A Men." Well, Mr. Click had one bad habit, he always sat by the front window and enjoyed his chewing tobacco. Naturally, he would spit out the window. If the preacher was long winded, which was usually the case, we boys would stay outside during the service. After running past the window, where Mr. Click sat, you didn't make the mistake again. Experience is a good teacher.

If Mr. Hopper was in attendance, we young folks would stay inside. We enjoyed watching him twirl his mustache. His technique was to obtain moisture from his mouth to get the twirl just right.

Before each service began, the preacher would always say, "Do what the spirit tells you." Mr. Hopper's wife, Aunt Marge, did her share of shouting. If encouraged by some hearty shouts of "A Men," she would preach a sermon. Under these conditions, who, in his right mind, would disagree with this type of service. Did you notice that I wrote preacher instead of pastor? We did have a pastor, but he only preached once a month. In the meantime, any preacher that came by, was called on to preach.

I was always thrilled by getting to church early so that I could stand on the porch and watch different people come up the road to church. One person, in particular, sticks out in my mind, and that was Mr. Carter for he always carried a Stamps Baxter songbook in his pocket.

At one time, I served as janitor at the church. Of course, it was necessary that I be early and get the building ready for service. On one such Sunday, my brother and cousin accompanied me. I got the building ready for service early with some extra time to spare. Well, we decided we would do a little practice preaching. We were in a big way of practice preaching, shouting, and "A Mening," when we discovered that we were not the only early birds that morning. It was none other than Mr. Click himself. Well, troublesome news traveled fast in those days. My father didn't attend service that Sunday, but the next morning he roused me from sleep with the warning not to let that happen again.

Over the years other things took place in our church. However, being of a derogatory nature, I feel they are not great memoires.

Today, I am always honored, to occasionally go by Liberty Baptist Church and observe the remodeling that has taken place. The members have managed to refurbish the sanctuary, an and add a fellowship hall. How such a small congregation has accomplished this task, must truly be the work of God.

Chapter 3

Politics

Politics is a necessity for every community, and at Brush Creek it was almost a second religion. Many arguments came about when the wife voted differently than the husband. In our community, there was more to politics than voting; the entertainment from speeches, the spotting of strange voting practices, and different types of campaigning.

When we young folks got word that Hoot Owl Taylor (not his real name) was to speak, you can bet that we were never late for his speech. Mr. Taylor was a regular office seeker, and occasionally he was successful in winning the office he was seeking. The most important part to Mr. Hoot Owl's election bid was his mode of entertainment, not his speaking ability. When speaking, he had the most unusual habit of taking frequent sips of water, which some folks thought the liquid in the large bottle was other than water. His speeches took place in the evening, and his mode of light was kerosene (coal oil) lanterns. Gnats would gather around these lanterns and quite often, in speaking Mr. Hoot would have a gnat land in his mouth, requiring a hasty drink of water. His favorite quote at the time was "I just baptized a gnat."

Now getting to the most important part,

or we boys thought so, was the dancing girls. It was necessary for Mr. Hoot to set up a temporary stage for the girls to dance on, of course the girls helped in the assembly of the stage. To see the girls working, in this fashion, we thought was a good lesson to learn. My cousin asked me, "Do you think these girls could hoe corn, feed the chickens, or slop the hogs?" I think that he was wondering, if in the future, this would be a good quality to keep in mind when looking for a wife. When the girls got the stage set up and began to dance, we boys fell into an exotic train of thought.

My grandfather was an office seeker, and his style of electioneering was the use of the jitney that served all the areas from Artemus to Kay Jay. The rear of the jitney had a small platform and from this he would throw candy to the children. He found this to be quite effective. The office he was seeking was the county judge (Judge executive today). I recall, after my grandfather had won the election, I accompanied my father to town (Barbourville); we went by my grandfather's office, and his secretary decided that I needed a kiss. I gave her quite a chase around the desk before she caught me. Those chasing days didn't last long.

When an election was to take place in our part of the county, we boys would visit outside the schoolhouse where the election was held. Several men would be milling around also. There were two things in particular that was puzzling to us: one was the table, at which one cast their vote, was located near an open window no matter how chilly the weather. The other was a list of voters tacked to a tree near the schoolhouse, some of the names on the list were residents of Brush Alford

Cemetery. I asked one of the men about these two observations. His answer, "seeing was believing" and the cemetery was "another local residence."

Chapter 4

In Search of A Bess Bug and The Elusive Snipe

We were fortunate to have neighbors who were always ready to lend a hand in any situation. One neighbor, in particular, was the Bruner Family. Dave Bruner, whom we lovingly referred to as Uncle Dave, was the Father and Husband of the Bruner family.

Many folk remedies were used for medical conditions in our area such as Castor Oil; a

I struck up a conversation with Uncle Dave. He informed me that one of the family had an earache and that a good remedy was a drop of blood from the Bess Bug. The ideal place for a Bess Bug to dwell was under a rotten log. He asked me if I knew where a rotten log could be located. Being familiar with the surrounding area, I remembered seeing a rotten log near the church. I accompanied my neighbor to the spot where the log was located. Upon arrival at the log he began to dig and soon found a Bess Bug. I often wondered if this remedy worked. I never thought to ask him, but I'm sure it did or he would have told me.

There was another bug which a couple of fellows said was easy to catch so after helping the neighbor catch the "Bug" of his choice, I felt, I had adequate experience to catch this bug. These fellows informed me that this bug was called a Snipe. One evening about dark they came by with a large bag. They told me that we would go Snipe hunting on the mountain above my house. As we started up the mountain, the fellows ask me to remain at the bottom of a hill holding the large bag, while they went on up the hill to locate a snipe. When they found the snipe, they would chase it down the hill. As the snipe came running down the hill they said it in would be very easy to catch it the large bag. After waiting about two hours and no snipe. I decided that I would stick to the Bess Bug hunting.

Chapter 5
Funeral For A Calf

Down near Barbourville on the Artemus Road, an astute lady by the name of Nola Minton raised fine horses and cattle. She also ran a small woodworking mill where she made several wooden objects.

Quite often, Mrs. Minton's fine horses would be in the Barbourville area parades. They were always one of the greatest attractions. Her cattle won many ribbons in the local fairs in the area.

One day, my father went by the Minton

house to inform our father of Popeye's death. He instructed us to take the calf to the lot below the barn and bury it. However, we felt Popeye should be given a fine burial and funeral since he was from a royal herd. I decided that I would do the honor of preaching Popeye's funeral. Preaching was not one of my gifts, but I had at one time practiced at church before starting time. My brother agreed that if I would do the preaching, that he would do the singing. After selecting a spot for the burial, we dug a grave. My brother sung a few songs after which I began to cite an obituary that I thought up. The obituary, as I recall went something like this: "born to a noble herd of fine cattle on a farm of prestige, moved to Brush Creek at an early age, lived in a barn of lowly esteem, but loved mightily by two boys who will miss him." Then I called on my brother to sing a few closing songs; one of which was the "Great Speckled

Bird." How he thought this was appropriate for Popeye I could never figure out. Then, I began my sermon. I can't remember all the honor I gave to Popeye, but I am sure it must have been good.

Later Mr. Click, who lived nearby said that he overheard the sacrilegious act we had given as a religious act for a calf. Again he said that my father would hear about this act.

Chapter 6

My Brother
Painting The Dog

Quite often it was necessary for my brother and me to find ways of entertainment. One way we had of entertaining ourselves was to roll old worn out automobile tires. We had one each. This is not bad within its self; it's where you roll it and why. One of our neighbor's mothers always rode a horse when she visited her daughter. We were out the news always got back to our parents about how well behaved we were. This always helped in gaining permission for other trips. However, on our way home from church that Sunday evening, our route took us past a cemetery. My cousin said one of the graves in the cemetery had a picture of the deceased on the tombstone. Well, at that particular time, this was a rarity worth investigating. Being curious boys, we decided to locate the grave for a look at the picture. By this time, it was around 9 o'clock. We did not have a light, but we had a few matches. Entering the cemetery, each of us went in a different direction, stopping along the way at various stones and striking a match in an attempt to locate the stone. Needless to say, we were unsuccessful in locating the grave with the picture on the stone. However, the next day the whole neighborhood was all abuzz about the strange lights flickering in the cemetery that night.

My brother got a bright idea one day. This was the day he decided to change the color of our dog. Our dog was a small white dog with black spots. He had taken the dog for a walk, and in doing so, he passed one of the neighbors who was painting with red paint. He got the bright idea, or so he thought, and this was to borrow enough red paint to paint the black spots on the dog. When he returned home that day with a big smile on his face, he thought he had accomplished something great. Well, my mother didn't think so; she was quite irate about the matter. The first thing that she did was to fill the washtub about half full of water and begin to try to wash off the red paint with soap. This was not successful. She then turned to the old faithful kerosene, which worked like trick.

Then she used linseed oil on the poor dog to stop the sting from the kerosene. While all this was taking place, my brother watched in nervous anticipation as his bright idea washed away, and dreading what was about to happen next. Spare the rod and spoil the child; that day the rod was not spared.

Chapter 7

The Old Elm Tree

One of our favorite places to gather was around the old Elm Tree, which stood near the railroad trestle. Beneath the drooping branches of the old elm, many debates, political gatherings, and tales were to be heard, but very few lies were told because we referred to the old elm tree as the Tree of Knowledge.

As I recall the topic of one debate was the

Gold Standard. What would happen to the future of our country if we went off the gold standard? My father opposed this idea; others thought it was a good idea. This debate took place in the evening when the work, if any, was finished for the day. It was debated for about two weeks, and had no bearing on the matter. Since then, our country did leave the gold standard, and our printing presses have been running at top speed. My father was often teased about his position on the gold standard, to which he often replied, it's not over yet."

One day my brother, cousin, and I were sitting on the roots of the old elm tree watching a model "A" Ford bouncing up the rough road towards the tree. When the driver spotted us, it came to a stop. The driver and his passenger exited the vehicle, came over to where we were sitting, and introduced themselves. The driver spoke first, "I" am A.B. (Happy) Chandler," and the other gentleman introduced himself as "Congressman Robinson." Needless to say, this made our day. At this time, the roads had begun to improve and the politicians were the first to make good use of them. The remainder of the day, we boys continued to sit under the old elm tree, wondering what dignitary might come by next.

The old elm tree had one outstanding characteristic that you seldom see on most elms. The roots of the gracious old elm had been worn slick by all the debaters that it had hosted over the years. If we could have coined and applicable phrase for this great tree, perhaps it would be "Knowledge starts here."

Not everything that happened at the old elm tree or nearby was of a positive nature.

I arrived one day for a day of learning, and to my amazement, no one was around. After spending some time sitting on the roots of the elm tree, I felt that a nap would be the appropriate thing to do. For my nap, I chose a place near the old elm tree, which was the railroad trestle. The railroad trestle was supported by stringers, or at least that's what we called them. At the bottom of these stringers was a large beam. I decided this would be my nap place. Just as I began to have pleasant dreams, I heard a lady's voice speaking words that did not become a lady, even the leaves on the elm began to curl up. This lady had a very pretty daughter, whom we boys referred to as "pretty as a speckled pup." It seems that as I was sleeping under the trestle, the irate lady's daughter was walking home from a friend's house. In order to get home, she needed to cross the trestle. The dear lady accused me of being wide awake and looking up at her daughter as she crossed the trestle. I tried to explain to her I was asleep. To this day when I tell this story, no one seems to believe me.

Chapter 8

Selling A Goat

One morning after a night of heavy rain, the creek overflowed its banks and quite a bit of refuse was floating by. We learned from this act of nature that after the water receded this would require some clean up. After looking at this mess, I was somewhat sad. I spied a beautiful white duck swimming. She seemed to be lost. I watched this beautiful duck off and on all day; she never left our property. I began to devise a plan to rescue this lovely jewel from the refuse. I was well aware at this time of my life that the chickens always came home to roost near nightfall; so I assumed the duck would do the same. Our barn was located below the road with the fence attached to each side of the barn front. This made a nice corner. So at nightfall, I sprinkled corn from the creek to the barn where the fence joined. It did not take very long for the duck to discover the corn. She ate her way to the corner of the barn fence, and at that time, I rushed in and caught the duck. I ran and showed my father the beautiful white duck. He suggested it would be a good project for us boys to try our hands at raising ducks; so he purchased us a mate for the duck. I did not feel the drake he chose did my lovely white duck justice, but he assured me that the drake was necessary. After some time, we had a nice flock of ducks. This did not set well with my mother. She was constantly complaining about where the ducks' choice of an outhouse. It was time for the ducks to go. My father knew a fellow who had a goat for sale. He told the fellow he thought his boys would trade a flock of ducks for his goat. This swap started a new adventure.

We soon found that this trade was not going to work. One morning, my brother went to get the goat out of the barn. The goat began to chase my brother, so he quickly ran to the ladder that went from the bottom floor of the barn to the loft. After a few minutes, he finally figured out the goat was not going to move from the bottom of the ladder; so he began to scream to get my mother's attention. Upon hearing my brother's despairing scream, my mother and I speedily ran to his rescue. After this unpleasant episode with my brother and the goat, my father suggested that we boys dispose of the goat. The poor goat had met his Waterloo.

We made a sign to advertise the sale of our goat for a dollar and fifty cents. One Saturday morning, we took the goat and the sign to the road above the house. About noonday, a car came by. It stopped, and we were overjoyed for the people in the car were a family by the name of Miller, who lived farther up Brush Creek. After the greetings and weather were out of the way, Mr. Miller said that his boys had four Rhode Island hens. The oldest boy spoke up and said, "We don't have any money, but we will gladly swap you the four hens for the goat." We gladly agreed to the deal and arranged the trade. I can't remember what happened

to the hens, but I do remember some good
chicken and dumplings.

Chapter 9

Man Kicked In The Head By A Mule

In our area, some strange accidents happened that required up to date surgery; or so we thought. One in particular was a fellow gearing up his mule to plow. The mule wanted the day off so he began to kick and act quite contrary; however, the fellow being behind the back part of the mule, tried to change the mule's attitude, so he gave the mule a swat with one of the plow lines. This action brought about a reaction from the mule in a swift kick to the fellow's head. The kick resulted in a hole the size of a silver dollar in the fellow's forehead. When the fellow arrived at the doctor's office, the doctor knew this required some sort of complicated surgery. At that moment, the doctor figured out the best thing was to take out the fractured bone. Then he proceeded to place a silver dollar over the hole and stitch the loose skin. I can attest to this procedure because this gentleman would always get off his mule and show us boys the odd indentation in his forehead. He did say that in stretching the skin over the mule kick, the doctor pulled the skin too tight. When he did this, it sort of misaligned his left ear. Come to think about it, his left ear was a little cockeyed.

One day, my brother saw one of the

neighbor's boys taking his mule to the creek to get a drink of water after a hard day of plowing. Well, I'm somewhat hesitant to say what my brother did; however, I thought the antic had some humor in it. My brother walked up behind the mule, who no doubt was enjoying drinking the cool water. My brother screamed as loud as he could, and the mule kicked up his hind legs, causing the boy to be thrown over the mule's head into the creek. The poor mule got spooked and ran for home, leaving the plow boy standing in the water. When my father learned about this caper, he asked my brother for an explanation. My brother's response was, after a hard day of plowing, the plow boy needed a bath.

One afternoon, one of our dear neighbors came by. He owned a fine mule, which he said, "was from the finest stock in Knox County." I could not understand this statement. The mule as I understand it, is a hybrid animal. While feeding his mule that afternoon, he casually reached the mule a nice clump of hay, and in so doing, his finger protruded in the mule's mouth resulting in a professional amputation. The moral of this story is to always know where your finger is.

Chapter 10

Pack Peddler

Pack Peddler was a title given to the many salesmen, who quite often came through our community. They sold small items such as beads, necklaces, small jewelry, and combs of all descriptions. One comb in particular was a fine toothcomb. It was used for none other than removing nits, which were lice from your hair.

I happened to be visiting our neighbors one

day, and I observed a fine toothcomb on the lady's dresser. At that time, we did not own a fine toothcomb, but we did have an occasional use for one. Since our family did not own a fine toothcomb, I decided to borrow this comb without permission of the lady of the house. The next day, the lady who owned the fine toothcomb came to our house. She informed my mother that, after I had left her house the previous day, she discovered that her fine toothcomb was missing. I readily admitted this error of judgment and felt that I was over compensated for this error.

My grandfather would occasionally tell about, a pack peddler, who came through the Greasy Creek area where he lived. The thing that impressed my grandfather the most was not the fellow's wares, but his large black moustache. On one of his peddling trips to Greasy Creek, the pack peddler's wares were

said, since sales were not the best that day, he was unable to buy dinner and he was very hungry. He asked my father, would he mind to call on his dear wife to prepare him a dinner? My father proceeded to bring the poor hungry fellow home with him. He asked my mother to prepare him a dinner. My mother was always able to cope with this sort of thing since my father was always bringing people home to eat with us. She began to cook a nice meal of fried ham, eggs, salad, beans, cornbread, some real butter, and a cup of coffee. She got out some of her best china: a plate, saucer, cup, and even put down one of her best dishrags for a cloth napkin. After placing the knife, fork, and spoon in the proper position, she asked father to invite the gentleman to the table. Meanwhile, my sister, brother, and I were watching to see how this fellow would eat his food. The first thing that he did was to throw that nice napkin down on the floor, and replace it with a dirty rag from his pocket. He pushed the knife, fork, and spoon away from his plate and reaching into another pocket, he pulled out a large Barlow knife to cut his meat and to eat his food with it. Needless to say, after the peddler finished his meal, my father quickly rushed him out of the house. After this dinner guest, my father became more choosey when it came to inviting strangers to dine at our home.

47

Chapter 11

Coal Mines

The coal mines in the Warren, Kay Jay, and Wheeler area became a source of employment for several families in the Brush Creek area. My father taught school and for extra income during the summer break, he would work at the mines.

The coalmines were highly unionized and quite often, they would strike and demand that their position be adapted.

One summer, a regional strike was called for several counties. This meant that all work must cease even the maintenance and upkeep of the mines. Well, it came to the attention of the Harlan County Union that the Kay Jay mines had a couple of fellows still on the payroll, looking after the upkeep and protection of the company property. One day the Harlan County Union came in mass and well armed even had machine guns. Meanwhile, the two fellows who were hired to look after the welfare of the Kay Jay mines went up the hill to check on the coal tipple and the coal loading area. One of the fellows was a devout Christian and minister of a local church in a nearby area. When the Harlan County Union arrived in the area of the Kay Jay mines, they set up their guns and aimed them at the treetops. They had been tipped off that the two fellows doing maintenance were headed up the hill to check the tipple. The minister's co-worker heard the bullets flying over the treetops. He said, "Preacher, it's time to pray." The minister replied, "There is a time to pray and a time to run, and this is a time to run."

Several stories have been told about strange objects being found among the coal in the mines. The most fascinating one, to me, was when some miners found a small man that had been embedded in the coal. During the night, the night shift cuts the coal using a coal cutting machine. This breaks the coal into small pieces, which the day shift loads into the tram cars. One morning as the miners began to load the coal into the tram cars, they found a small petrified man about four feet tall, that had been dislodged from the coal by the cutting machine. This small petrified man had been embedded in the seam of coal since is formation.

Chapter 12

The Forbidden Fruit

One lovely day, my brother, cousin and I decided we would go fishing. My cousin remarked that he knew the ideal spot. So we went to our favorite place to dig worms. After digging the worms, we gathered up our fishing gear, nothing fancy, just a cane pole with hook, line, and sinker attached. With this type of equipment, it was obvious. We were not going to get a record catch. However, we did let some large ones get away.

After gathering our gear, we proceeded to our cousin's ideal fishing spot, and by all indications, it did look good. In the middle of this spot, a drift of small logs and debris had become stuck to the bottom. We began fishing by casting our lines next to the drift having no luck at all. During this time, I spotted a beautiful apple tree across the creek with the most lovely crop of June apples you have ever looked upon. I remarked to my fishing partners, "those sure look tempting." My cousin reminded me of Adam and Eve's punishment; when Eve picked the forbidden apple and let Adam have a bite. I could not remember this story. Since my cousin was more attentive in church, I figured he knew what he was talking about. I asked him, "What happened?" He said, "Adam took such a large bite that it became lodged in his throat, protruding out as a small knot. This is why we fellows have a knot on our throat, which is called an Adam's apple."

With no luck fishing, we began to devise a plan to borrow a few of those apples. In order to get the apples, we would have to get across the creek. Now this presented a problem, so our plan was return after dark, pull off our clothes, and cross the creek in the nude.

After dark, we set our plan into motion. We arrived at the creek, removed our clothes, and waded across the creek in the nude. When we got to the apple tree, we discovered that we could not reach the apples. At this point, my brother said that he would climb the tree and shake off a few of the apples. He began to shake the tree and sure enough, the apples began to fall. My cousin and I became so excited that we began to talk too loud. The owner heard the noise and sent his sons to see what was happening. We heard them coming across the field and fast approaching the apple tree. We immediately went back across the creek forgetting about my brother, who was still up the apple tree in the nude. The owner's sons were not impressed upon finding my nude brother in the apple tree. After getting back across the creek, my cousin knew we had to do something to get my brother out of the tree. As luck would have it, we discovered a pile of rocks near the spot where we had waded the creek. We began to throw rocks at my brother's captors. Being under a hail of stones, they began to high tail it home. The next day, the owner of the apple tree came to see my father. This did not set well with my father so he applied some corrective action. Later, we were not able to sit well either.

Chapter 13

Uncle Tom's Store

In most of the rural areas, such as Brush Creek there was a local store, which sold many staples necessary for sustaining a rural community. Uncle Tom's store sold canned goods, which were limited because at that time very few foods were processed in cans. Apple cider was a favorite of the men folk on slow days of which there were many due to the lack of work or the resistance to work.

On these days, the men would gather at the store and enjoy a cup of cider and a soda cracker. The store sold soda crackers, which were shipped loosely packed in large wooden barrels. Cattle feed, nails, and candy were shipped in smaller barrels called kegs. In later years of the stores existence other items were added such as: kerosene (coal oil), ladies dresses and everyone's favorite, the famous Moon Pie. As the needs of the community changed so did the little country store.

Uncle Tom was an outstanding man in many ways. In his brogan shoes, he was six foot tall, slim and neatly dressed. His mode of dress consisted of bow tie, white shirt, dress pants, and arm bands. In those days lots of fellows wore the elastic arm bands above the elbows to adjust the length of their shirt sleeves. We might say that one size fits all.

Uncle Tom did have a few habits that

were considered normal in that day. He was never without his chew of tobacco and the juice that seem to collect at the corners of his mouth. On winter days, all the local men would gather around the warm pot bellied stove, which stood in the middle of the store and spit their tobacco juice in the fire. It was said that on one such occasion the spitting of tobacco juice was so frequent that the fire was extinguished. Uncle Tom believed in keeping healthy and for this purpose he kept a gallon of moonshine with a small root of gin sing floating in the jug. This Tonic as he called it was used several times daily for good health.

Some of the products that were sold in the store should have been recalled, if you used the standards of today, but whoever heard of recalling in that day and time. One product in particular was apple cider. One month its shipment was interrupted by mechanical problems in the jitney. After sitting in the hot July sun for a few days it finally arrived at the store. When the men in the community heard that the cider had finally arrived, they gathered at the store one Saturday afternoon to socialize and drink cider. This cider seemed to be different. After several cups, it seemed obvious that they had become intoxicated. It has been said that several prominent male members of the local church had hangover the following Sunday.

Uncle Tom was accused of creating a shortage of chickens in our community. One day a traveling salesman came by Uncle Tom's store. He claimed that he was from New York and in his buggy; he had all the latest New York styles in ladies' dresses. Excitedly, Uncle Tom bought all the dresses the salesman had. When the ladies heard about the dresses, they came by the store to see and inquire about prices. Knowing that the ladies didn't have ready cash, he informed them that six fat hens was the price of regular dresses and eight fat hens was the price of lace trimmed dresses. That was one time all the ladies in the community wore the latest New York styles. Uncle Tom took the hens to the Fair Grounds near Barbourville, and was able to sell the hens at a profit. Needless to say not everyone was happy, the wives husbands had to replenish the flocks and the roosters had nothing to do but crow.

Chapter 14

School Days

Our school building consisted of one large room and two unattached small buildings known as out houses. All six grades were segmented by grades. During the day, the teacher would call each grade to the front benches and go over the lesson. When the lesson was over, the students would return to their individual seats. In the winter months, a pot bellied stove was used for heating the room. Air conditioning was fresh air, which blew through the open windows. A table in the rear of the room was used for a water bucket and individual glasses for the students to drink from. During the winter months, a local student was hired to build a fire in the stove about thirty minutes before school started. This student also was responsible for drawing water from the well and placing it on the table for drinking purposes. The student that was hired to do these chores was paid by the teacher at the rate of five cents per day. On Friday of each week, the teacher swept the room in preparation for the following Monday morning.

One school term in our area, a lovely lady was hired to teach. The sixth graders decided it would be very funny to play a few tricks on the new teacher. While they were at recess one day, they spied a big black snake sunning on a log. They killed the black snake and coiled it up in the drawer of the teacher's desk with the head pointed toward the person who opened the drawer. At the end of recess, the teacher sat down at her desk, pulled open the drawer, and was face to face with the snake. She almost fainted. Upon her recovery, she made several threats of severe punishment when she found the guilty students, and she would find out for these two sixth graders had other antics in store for her. Near the school, upon the hill was a cool fresh water spring, which was used by the teacher and students to keep their lunch milk cool. During recess on day these two sixth graders were thinking naughty thoughts while they were playing in the vicinity of the spring. A new idea was in the making when they spotted a small bull frog. They caught the frog and placed it in the teacher's milk container. At the end of the school term, the lovely teacher announced that she would not be back. The two sixth graders could not understand this decision by the teacher.